CLASSIC RECIPES

Delectable
Desserts

simple
and
delicious
food

Wendy Hobson

ARCTURUS

ARCTURUS

This edition published in 2013 by Arcturus Publishing Limited
26/27 Bickels Yard, 151–153 Bermondsey Street,
London SE1 3HA

ISBN: 978-1-78212-015-5
AD002582US

Printed in China

Contents

Introduction

We all know that a balanced and healthy diet should focus on fruits and vegetables, protein, and unrefined carbs to make sure we get all the vitamins and other nutrients our bodies need to stay healthy. That's a given. But it's not the whole picture because—as the old adage goes—a little of what you fancy does you good!

Every now and again, we all need a treat; something delightfully sweet and even a little wicked! The fact that we don't have sweet things every day makes it that much more special when we do. So this book offers you a collection of mouth-watering treats for that very special corner of our diet when we can really indulge ourselves: delectable desserts.

In our busy lives, it's unusual for most of us to have the time to make desserts to follow everyday meals. Perhaps we choose a pot of yogurt, some ice-cream or a piece of fruit, but what we might call 'proper' desserts are reserved for weekends and for entertaining.

There is such a vast array of wonderful desserts to choose from in our international cuisine that there really is something for everyone. Each region has its own favorites, from the pies and tarts of the US to the honey-drenched pastries of the Middle East or the fresh fruit concoctions of the Mediterranean.

For summer days or outside events, you might choose a light and refreshing fruit salad, but for those cold winter evenings, some old-fashioned comfort food hits the spot: a rice pudding or a steamed pudding. A dinner party for business colleagues requires something stylish, such as a lemon tart, while a bread and butter pudding would suit a family event.

Then there is that most versatile of desserts, the crêpe—so often just rolled up with a squeeze of lemon juice—which here is transformed into a wonderful wine-soaked delight.

Even the most sophisticated of the recipes here is not difficult to create in your own kitchen. All the ingredients in these recipes are readily available, and the methods are clear and step-by-step so even a beginner will be able to follow them through to great results.

Choosing your desserts

For every day or for weekends, you will probably just opt for the dessert that most takes your fancy, but for a dinner party or a special meal, it is worth giving your choice a little more thought.

Start by selecting your main course—will it be meat, fish, or vegetarian; baked, roasted, or fried; light and summery or rich and robust for a cold winter evening? That will set the tone for the overall occasion, and you can keep that in mind as your style, then choose your side dishes to complement the main course in flavor, color, texture, and cooking method.

Think about those elements for each choice you make, and then for each course as you add it to your menu. That way you won't end up with too many things of the same color (chicken, potato and cauliflower will not look stunning), or cooked in a similar way (steak pie followed by mince pie is not good). Contrast and balance will give you the best culinary experience.

That is particularly important when you reach your dessert choice because it is the grand finale of your meal. Your guests will already have eaten one or two courses, so they are no longer hungry; the dessert is something to savor. Avoid a pastry dessert if you have already served a pie, and choose a fruit or perhaps a chocolate option. If your main course was deliciously rich, perhaps a light, fruity dessert would fit the bill.

So work your way through this great collection and enjoy these sumptuous desserts with your family and friends.

Crème brûlée

A creamy custard with a subtle flavor, this is a dessert that should be served in delicate dishes or ramekins. I like to garnish it with a few brightly colored soft fruits and a couple of mint leaves.

Serves 4

4 egg yolks
2 tsp superfine sugar
1 tbsp vanilla extract
450ml/¾pt/2 cups light cream
2 tbsp demerara sugar, plus extra for sprinkling
1 tbsp confectioner's sugar

To serve
A few raspberries
A few mint leaves

1. Beat the egg yolks with the sugar and vanilla until well blended.
2. Put the cream in a heatproof bowl set over a pan of gently simmering water and stir until warm.
3. Stir in the egg yolk mixture and heat very gently, stirring regularly, for about 10–12 minutes until the mixture coats the back of a spoon. Do not allow it to boil.
4. Strain the custard into individual bowls, cover, and leave in the fridge to chill for a few hours or, preferably, overnight.
5. Fill the broiler pan with very cold water or ice and stand the bowls in the cold water. Flash quickly under a very hot broiler until the sugar caramelizes, or use a culinary blow torch.
6. Chill for several hours before serving decorated with mint and raspberries, and a sprinkling of confectioner's sugar.

Serves 4

For the meringues
4 egg whites
225g/8oz/1 cup
superfine sugar

For the custard
4 egg yolks
50g/2oz/¼ cup superfine
sugar
300ml/½pt/1¼ cups
light cream
1 vanilla bean, split
lengthways

To decorate
Clear honey or
maple syrup

Floating islands

A classic nursery dessert, this has light and fluffy islands of meringue—
crunchy on the outside and just slightly chewy in the center—lightly drizzled
with honey and floating on a lake of smooth custard.

1. Heat the oven to its lowest setting and line
a cookie sheet with waxed paper.
2. To make the meringues, whisk the egg
whites until stiff, then gradually whisk in half
the sugar. Gently fold in the remaining sugar
using a metal spoon.
3. Spoon 4 large or 8 small ovals of meringue
on to the cookie sheet. Pull a knife across
the islands so they are slightly ridged.
4. Place in the bottom of the oven for about
1½ hours.
5. Turn the meringues on to their sides and
return to the oven for a further 30 minutes
to 1½ hours, depending on their size
and the heat of your oven, until they have
completely dried. Remove and leave to cool.

6. Meanwhile, to make the custard, mix the
egg yolks and sugar in a bowl with a wooden
spoon until well blended.
7. Heat the cream and vanilla in a pan to just
boiling. Whisk a little cream into the eggs,
then gradually whisk in the remainder.
8. Pour into a heatproof bowl set over a pan of
simmering water and stir gently for
10 minutes until thick, taking care the
mixture doesn't boil.
9. Remove from the heat and strain into a
bowl. Scrape the vanilla seeds into the
custard, then cover and cool.
10. When ready to serve, pour the custard into
a bowl and float the meringues on top.
Drizzle with honey to or syrup serve.

Lemon sorbet

Serves 4

450g/1lb/2 cups superfine sugar
600ml/1pt/2½ cups water
6 lemons
A few mint leaves

Offer lemon sorbet as a fresh summer dessert, or as tiny portions in espresso cups to cleanse the palate after a rich main course and before dessert. You don't have to serve it in lemon skins, but that does make a splendid display.

1. Put the sugar and water in a pan and heat gently until the sugar dissolves. Increase the heat and boil gently for 2 minutes.
2. Meanwhile, cut the top third off each lemon and scoop out the flesh using a grapefruit knife or a teaspoon so that you keep 4 of the shells intact.
3. Remove the syrup from the heat and squeeze in the lemon juice. Grate the zest of one of the extra lemons and add it to the syrup. Leave to cool.
4. If you have an ice-cream maker, churn the liquid until firm. If not, pour the mixture into a shallow freezer container and put into the freezer. Remove and stir to break up the ice crystals after 2 hours, then 4 hours, then leave to freeze. The lemon shells can go into the freezer at the same time.
5. Grate the zest of the second extra lemon into shreds.
6. An hour before you are ready to serve, remove the sorbet from the freezer and leave to soften slightly. Spoon into the lemon shells and serve decorated with mint leaves and the remaining lemon zest.

Apple strudel

A European dish, strudel formerly did not feature in cookery books because making the pastry successfully was too difficult. How lucky we are to have chilled and frozen filo pastry at our fingertips!

Serves 4

For the strudel

700g/1½lb dessert apples, peeled, cored and chopped

100g/4oz/½ cup superfine sugar

Grated zest and juice of ½ orange

Freshly grated nutmeg

8 sheets filo pastry

50g/2oz/¼ cup butter, melted

Confectioner's sugar

To serve

Custard (page 8)

1. Heat the oven to 190°C/375°F/ Gas 5 and grease a cookie sheet.
2. Put the apples, sugar, and orange zest and juice into a pan. Grate a little nutmeg over the top, then stir everything gently together.
3. Place a sheet of waxed paper on the work surface and lay a sheet of filo on it. Brush with the melted butter, then place another sheet on top. Continue until you have used all the sheets.
4. Spoon the apple over the pastry, keeping it away from the edges, then carefully roll and fold the pastry to make a long sausage shape, using the waxed paper to help. Brush with the remaining melted butter, then lift the strudel on the paper carefully on to the cookie sheet.
5. Bake in the oven for about 20 minutes until lightly golden.
6. To serve hot or cold, sprinkle with confectioner's sugar and serve with custard, if liked.

Summer pudding

Use a mixture of summer fruits for this luscious dessert, such as strawberries, raspberries, redcurrants, blackcurrants, blackberries, and cherries. Don't include too many blackcurrants or their flavor will dominate the dish.

Serves 4

700g/1½lb mixed
soft fruits

2 tbsp fresh orange juice

100g/4oz/½ cup
superfine sugar

8 thick slices of stale
bread, crusts removed

To serve

Soured cream or heavy
cream, whipped

1. Remove any hulls or pits from the fruit. Cut any large fruit in halves or quarters so that it is all roughly the same size.
2. Put the fruit in a pan with the orange juice and sugar over a low heat and stir occasionally until the sugar has dissolved and the fruit is just soft but not soggy. Remove from the heat. Spoon 2–3 tbsp of juice into a bowl and put aside.
3. While the fruit is cooking, use 7 slices of bread to line a 900ml/1½pt/3¾ cup pudding basin, cutting it to fit.
4. Spoon the warm fruit into the bread-lined bowl, then cut the remaining slice to fit and place it on the top.
5. Place a saucer that fits inside the basin on top of the pudding so that it presses down on it. Place a can or other weight on top and chill overnight in the fridge.
6. Before serving, remove the saucer and weight. Put a serving dish on top and invert the pudding on to it. Spoon the reserved juice over to cover any bread that is not soaked in fruit juice.
7. Serve with soured cream or whipped cream.

Baklava

Popular throughout the Middle East in various guises, these delicious honey and nut pastries are very sweet, so it's a good idea to cut them into small squares for serving.

Serves 4

350g/12oz/1 pack filo pastry
75g/3oz/⅓ cup butter, melted

For the syrup

450g/1lb/2 cups superfine sugar
450ml/¾pt/2 cups water
1 cinnamon stick
1 tbsp lemon juice

For the filling

225g/8oz/2 cups almonds, finely chopped
100g/4oz/1 cup walnuts, finely chopped
50g/2oz/¼ cup superfine sugar
3 tbsp fine breadcrumbs
1 tsp ground cinnamon
A pinch of ground cloves

1. Heat the oven to 160°C/325°F/Gas 3 and grease and line a 28cm/11in baking pan. Keep the filo pastry covered in plastic wrap or a damp tea towel when you are not using it so that it doesn't dry out and go crumbly.

2. Put all the syrup ingredients in a pan and heat gently, stirring occasionally, until the sugar has dissolved. Bring to the boil and simmer for about 8 minutes until thick, without stirring. Remove from the heat and leave to cool.

3. Mix together all the filling ingredients.

4. Place a sheet of filo in the pan, brush with melted butter, then put another sheet on top. Continue in this way until you have half the filo sheets in the tin.

5. Spoon the filling over the pastry and smooth it flat.

6. Layer the remaining pastry on top, brushing each one with melted butter, including the top layer. Trim the edges if you wish.

7. Take a very sharp knife and score through the pastry to mark it out into small squares or diamond shapes.

8. Bake in the oven for about 1 hour until golden and crisp. Cover with a sheet of foil if the top is becoming too brown.

9. Remove from the oven and, while still hot, spoon the syrup over the baklava. Leave for 5–6 hours so that the syrup soaks in.

10. Cut into squares, as marked, and serve.

Don't be too constrained by details when making a fruit salad, just use the fruits that are the best at the time—ripe, fresh and juicy. For an Italian-style salad, cut the fruit into quite small pieces and marinate it in sweet Marsala or liqueur.

Italian fresh fruit salad

Serves 4

For the syrup
Juice of 1 lemon
50g/2oz/¼ cup superfine sugar
5 tbsp Marsala or a sweet liqueur

For the fruit salad
2 dessert apples
2 pears
1 tbsp lemon juice
1 orange
2 kiwi fruit
1 pomegranate
225g/8oz strawberries

1. Put the lemon juice, sugar, and Marsala or liqueur in a small pan over a low heat, stirring occasionally until the sugar has dissolved. Bring to the boil, then remove from the heat and leave to cool.
2. To prepare the fruit, cut it into small, even-sized pieces. Core and chop the apples and pears, removing the skin only if it is tough. Place in a bowl and toss with the lemon juice to stop it from discoloring. Peel and chop the orange and kiwi. Halve the pomegranate and scoop out the seeds. Hull and chop the strawberries.
3. Put all the fruits in the bowl with the apples and pears.
4. Pour the cooled syrup over and stir gently. Cover and chill for several hours, if possible, before serving.

Chocolate mousse

You will get the best flavor if you use good-quality chocolate that contains at least 70 per cent cocoa solids. It will cost a little more but it will be well worth it. You might prefer a few raspberries, or perhaps a little cream, with your mousse.

Serves 4

225g/8oz good-quality semi-sweet chocolate, broken into pieces
25g/1oz/2 tbsp unsalted butter
4 eggs, separated
A pinch of salt

To decorate
A few strawberries
A few mint leaves

1. Melt the chocolate and butter in a heatproof bowl set over a pan of gently simmering water, stirring occasionally. Once melted, remove the bowl from the heat and leave to cool for a few minutes.
2. Meanwhile, whisk the egg whites with the salt in a clean, grease-free bowl until they form soft peaks.
3. Lightly whisk the egg yolks, then stir into the cooled chocolate.
4. Using a metal spoon, stir a spoonful of the egg whites into the chocolate, then fold in the remainder, keeping the mixture as light as possible.
5. Chill for 1–2 hours in the fridge until set.
6. Serve decorated with strawberries and mint leaves.

Peach melba

Created in honor of Dame Nellie Melba, the Australian opera singer, this is a dish of peaches poached in wine, combined with ice-cream and raspberry coulis. Sometimes it is sprinkled with slivered almonds.

Serves 4

250ml/8fl oz/1 cup dessert wine
600ml/1pt/2½ cups water
100g/4oz/½ cup superfine sugar
1 vanilla bean, split
4 peaches, halved and pitted
200g/7oz raspberries
2 tbsp confectioner's sugar
4 scoops of vanilla ice-cream

To decorate
150ml/¼pt/⅔ cup whipped cream (optional)
4 candied cherries (optional)

1. Put the wine, water, and sugar in a pan, add the vanilla bean, and bring slowly to the boil, stirring until the sugar has dissolved.
2. Add the peaches and simmer, keeping the heat low, for about 20 minutes until soft. Leave to cool slightly.
3. Remove the peach skins and slice the flesh into wedges, then put them back in the syrup and leave to cool completely.
4. Purée the raspberries and confectioner's sugar in a processor or with a hand blender. If you prefer a seedless sauce, rub the sauce through a sieve.
5. To assemble the dessert, spoon the peaches and ice-cream into sundae glasses with a little of the raspberry coulis. Top with cream and cherries, if liked, and serve the remaining raspberry coulis separately.

Lemon tart

The sharp, fresh flavor of lemon is the perfect choice to follow a rich main course, such as a beef casserole in wine. It needs nothing more than a few fresh mint leaves to display it at its best.

Serves 4

For the pie crust

225g/8oz/2 cups all-purpose flour, plus extra for sprinkling

1 tbsp superfine sugar

A pinch of salt

50g/2oz/¼ cup vegetable shortening

50g/2oz/¼ cup butter

1 egg yolk

About 50ml/2fl oz/¼ cup cold water

For the filling

6 eggs

Grated zest and juice of 6 lemons

200g/7oz/scant 1 cup superfine sugar

100g/4oz/½ cup butter, diced

To decorate

A few mint leaves

2 tsp confectioner's sugar (optional)

1. Heat the oven to 190°C/375°F/Gas 5 and put a baking sheet in the oven. Grease and line a 23cm/9in tart pan.
2. Put the flour, sugar, and salt in a bowl and rub in the shortening and butter until the mixture resembles breadcrumbs; alternatively, use the food processor. Add the egg yolk, then gradually add the water, mixing with a knife or pulsing the processor until the mixture begins to bind together.
3. Tip out on to a lightly floured surface and shape into a smooth ball; do not overwork. Roll it out to a round and use to line the prepared pan. Cover with a sheet of waxed paper and fill with baking beans.
4. Place the pan on the hot baking sheet and bake in the oven for 10 minutes. Remove the beans and paper and return the tart shell to the oven for 5 minutes until just lightly golden. Put to one side to cool.
5. Meanwhile, put the eggs, lemon juice, and sugar in a pan over a low heat and whisk continuously until thick. Strain into a clean bowl and stir in the butter until melted.
6. Spoon the filling into the pastry case and leave to cool, then chill until set.
7. Serve garnished with mint leaves and sprinkled with sifted confectioner's sugar, if liked.

Pecan pie

This is a sweet and sticky recipe from the South that shows off pecan nuts to perfection. Use dark corn syrup if you can; if it is not available, three-quarters light corn syrup with one-quarter molasses is a good substitute.

Serves 4–6

For the pastry

100g/4oz/1 cup all-purpose flour, plus extra for dusting

½ tsp salt

1 tsp superfine sugar

75g/3oz/⅓ cup vegetable shortening

3 tbsp cold water

For the filling

175g/6oz/1½ cups pecans

3 eggs

250ml/8fl oz/1 cup dark corn syrup

75g/3oz/⅓ cup superfine sugar

75g/3oz/⅓ cup dark brown sugar

A pinch of salt

1 tsp vanilla extract

75g/3oz/⅓ cup butter, melted

To serve

Whipped cream or crème fraîche

1. Heat the oven to 220°C/425°F/Gas 7 and grease and line a 20cm/8in flan ring.
2. Put the flour, salt, and sugar in a bowl or a food processor. Rub in the vegetable shortening until the mixture resembles breadcrumbs, then gradually add enough cold water to mix to a smooth dough.
3. Roll out on a lightly floured surface and use to line the prepared flan ring. Place in the fridge while you make the filling.
4. Chop 100g/4oz/1 cup of the pecans.
5. Whisk the eggs until light, then whisk in the corn syrup, both sugars, the salt, and the vanilla extract.
6. Stir in the melted butter and the chopped pecans.
7. Spoon into the pastry case and arrange the remaining pecan halves on top.
8. Reduce the oven temperature to 180°C/350°F/Gas 4 and bake in the oven for about 45 minutes until the center is just firm to the touch and the top is golden and set.
9. Serve warm or cold with a spoonful of cream or crème fraîche.

Raspberry pavlova

Unlike a traditional meringue, pavlova includes cornstarch and vinegar and bakes to a softer, marshmallow texture. This is a grown-up version. If you are serving to the family, omit the liqueur or use plain cream and serve the flavored cream separately.

Serves 4–6

For the meringue

4 egg whites

225g/8oz/1 cup superfine sugar

½ tsp white wine vinegar

½ tsp vanilla extract

1 tsp cornstarch

For the filling

600ml/1pt/2¼ cups heavy cream

3–4 tbsp confectioner's sugar

1 tsp Cointreau or other fruit liqueur (optional)

450g/1lb raspberries

1. Heat the oven to 150°C/300°F/Gas 2.
2. Take a large sheet of waxed paper. Drawing round a plate or dish, mark a 20cm/8in circle on the paper, then turn it over and place it on a large baking sheet. You should be able to see the circle underneath.
3. Whisk the egg whites in a clean, grease-free bowl until they form soft peaks.
4. Whisk in the sugar a little at a time until the mix is smooth and glossy, then fold in the remaining sugar with a metal spoon.
5. Gently fold in the wine vinegar, vanilla, and cornstarch.
6. Spoon the mixture on to the waxed paper, using your pencil guide to make a circle and piling the meringue up at the sides to make a rough bowl shape.
7. Bake in the oven for 1 hour until crisp on the outside. Leave to cool on a wire rack.
8. Whip the cream until stiff, then stir in the sugar and Cointreau or liqueur, if liked. Continue to whip until the cream is stiff. Spoon into the pastry shell and arrange the raspberries on top. Serve immediately after assembling.

Serves 4

For the profiteroles
75g/3oz/⅓ cup butter, cut into pieces
175ml/6fl oz/¾ cup water
A pinch of salt
100g/4oz/1 cup all-purpose flour
3 eggs

For the filling
450ml/¾pt/2 cups whipping cream

For the chocolate sauce
200g/7oz semi-sweet chocolate
90ml/3fl oz/6 tbsp water
75g/3oz/⅓ cup superfine sugar
1 tbsp brandy (optional)

Profiteroles with chocolate sauce

Piled high in a bowl with whipped cream tantalizingly glimpsed through the cracks in the soft pastry and drizzled with sticky satin chocolate sauce, this is too good to be saved for special occasions.

1. Heat the oven to 400°C/200°F/Gas 6 and grease a large cookie sheet. Put the butter, water, and salt in a pan, bring to the boil.
2. Remove from the heat, tip in all the flour, and beat for a few minutes until the mixture is smooth.
3. Return to a minimum heat and beat for 30 seconds, then remove from the heat and leave to cool for 1 minute.
4. Beat in the eggs one at a time until the dough is shiny and soft.
5. Spoon the pastry into a piping bag and pipe about 20 small balls on to the cookie sheet.
6. Bake in the oven for about 20 minutes until puffed and golden.
7. Remove from the oven and split the profiteroles horizontally to release the steam. Arrange on a wire rack to cool.
8. Meanwhile, whip the cream until stiff.
9. Melt the chocolate, water, and sugar together over a low heat. Simmer for 1 minute until slightly thickened. Stir in the brandy, if liked.
10. When the profiteroles are cold, fill with the cream and pile on to a serving dish. Pour the chocolate sauce over and serve at once.

Crêpes suzette

The simple pancake is so amazingly versatile. It can be anything from a quick breakfast or a street snack to a sophisticated dinner-party dessert—the chameleon of dessert recipes. Here, it is at its most sophisticated.

Serves 4

For the crêpes
100g/4oz/1 cup all-purpose flour
A pinch of salt
3 eggs
250ml/8fl oz/1 cup milk
100g/4oz/½ cup butter, melted

For the sauce
375ml/13fl oz/1½ cups orange juice
2 tsp grated orange zest
2 tbsp superfine sugar
1 tsp Cointreau
3 oranges, peeled and cut into segments

1. Put the flour and salt into a bowl and make a well in the center.
2. Add the eggs and whisk until blended, then gradually add half the milk and half the melted butter, whisking all the time to make sure the batter is smooth. Gradually whisk in enough of the remaining milk to give the consistency of light cream. Leave to stand for 30 minutes.
3. Heat a little of the remaining butter in a pancake pan. Rotate the pan as you add a spoonful of the batter so that it spreads thinly over the base of the pan. Fry over a medium heat until set on top and beginning to brown underneath.
4. Turn or toss the crêpe and cook the other side for a minute until browned. Keep the crêpe warm while you cook the remainder.
5. Put the orange juice and zest and sugar in a pan and heat gently until the sugar has dissolved. Bring to the boil and boil for 5 minutes.
6. Add the Cointreau and oranges.
7. Pour a little of the sauce into the pancake pan over a very low heat and add a crêpe. Turn in the sauce, then fold into quarters and push to the side of the pan. Repeat with the remaining pancakes. You will probably have to do a few at a time, then transfer them to a serving plate to keep warm until you are ready to serve.

Traditionally, this is made with white bread, cut into triangles, with the crusts removed, which is a delicious option but not the only one. I like to keep the crusts on, and often make it with wholemeal bread or even brioche for a really rich option.

Bread and butter pudding

Serves 4

50g/2oz/¼ cup butter
10–12 slices bread
75g/3oz/½ cup golden raisins
½ tsp ground cinnamon
350ml/12fl oz/1⅓ cups milk
50 ml/2fl oz/¼ cup heavy cream
2 eggs
30g/1oz/2 tbsp superfine sugar
Freshly grated nutmeg

1. Grease a deep ovenproof dish.
2. Spread the butter on the bread and cut into triangles or small rectangles, as you prefer. Layer in the prepared dish, butter-side up, sprinkling with the raisins and cinnamon in between the slices.
3. Gently heat the milk and cream to just below boiling point. Meanwhile, whisk the eggs and sugar until pale and light.
4. Pour the milk and cream into the eggs, whisking continuously, then slowly pour the mixture over the bread, allowing it time to soak in. Grate some nutmeg over the top.
5. Leave to stand and soak for a few minutes while you heat the oven to 180°C/350°F/Gas 4.
6. Bake the pudding in the oven for about 40 minutes until golden and crispy on the top and slightly springy when pressed. If it starts to look too browned on top before it is ready, cover it with waxed paper or foil for the end of the cooking time.

Sticky toffee pudding

These little puddings get their rich toffee flavor from sugar, molasses and dates. You can make individual puddings, or put the mixture in one large dish, in which case steam for about 45 minutes. You can also bake them in a moderate oven.

Serves 4

For the pudding

225g/8oz/1⅓ cups dates, pitted and finely chopped
175ml/6fl oz/¾ cup boiling water
75g/3oz/⅓ cup butter
150g/5oz/⅔ cup soft brown sugar
2 eggs, lightly beaten
2 tbsp light corn syrup
175g/6oz/1½ cups self-rising flour
1 tsp baking soda
100ml/3½fl oz/scant ½ cup milk
1 tsp vanilla extract

For the sauce

175g/6oz/¾ cup light brown sugar
50g/2oz/¼ cup butter, diced
250ml/8fl oz/1 cup heavy cream
2 tbsp molasses or dark corn syrup

1. Put the dates in a bowl and pour the boiling water over. Leave to stand for 30 minutes while you prepare the remaining ingredients.
2. Grease four 300ml/½pt/1¼ cup pudding basins.
3. Cream the butter and sugar until light and creamy. Gradually whisk in the eggs and syrup, beating well as you do so.
4. Fold in half the flour with the baking powder, then some of the milk. Continue adding the flour and milk alternately until they are all blended to a smooth batter.
5. Add the vanilla to the dates then pour them into the mixture, including any water that has not soaked in, and stir until well blended.
6. Pour the mixture into the prepared basins, cover with foil or baking parchment and arrange a large saucepan. Fill with boiling water to come half way up the sides of the basins, cover and steam for 25 minutes.
7. Meanwhile, melt the sugar, butter, and half the cream over a low heat, stirring until the sugar has dissolved. Raise the heat and bring to the boil, then stir in the molasses and simmer for 2 minutes. Remove from the heat and cool for a few minutes before stirring in the remaining cream.
8. Leave the puddings to cool in the basins for a few minutes, then turn out on to serving plates and pour the sauce over to serve.

Serves 4

For the pudding
150g/5oz/1¼ cups all-purpose flour
1 tsp baking powder
2 tbsp unsweetened chocolate powder
100g/4oz/½ cup superfine sugar
1 egg, lightly beaten
120ml/4fl oz/⅓ cup milk
50g/2oz/¼ cup sweet butter, melted

For the sauce
2 tbsp unsweetened chocolate powder
150g/5oz/¾ cup soft brown sugar
300ml/½pt/1¼ cups boiling water

To serve
1 tbsp confectioner's sugar
Whipped cream

Gooey chocolate pudding

This baked dessert is a cross between a pudding and a brownie, baking to a lovely, light top with a gooey, sauce-like layer beneath. All it needs is a sprinkling of confectioner's sugar and a dollop of cream for a chocoholic's heaven.

1. Heat the oven to 180°C/350°F/Gas 4 and grease a deep, 23cm/9in ovenproof dish.
2. Mix the flour, baking powder, unsweetened chocolate, and sugar in a bowl.
3. Combine the egg, milk, and butter and whisk together, then stir into the dry ingredients and mix to a smooth dough. Spoon into the prepared dish and level the top.
4. For the sauce, mix together the unsweetened chocolate and brown sugar and sprinkle over the pudding. Carefully pour the just-boiled water over the top.
6. Place in the oven and bake for about 40 minutes until the cake is set on top and a skewer inserted halfway into the center comes out clean.
7. Put the confectioner's sugar in a fine sieve or tea strainer and sprinkle over the top. Serve with whipped cream.

Steamed syrup pudding

Serves 4

3 tbsp light corn syrup
175g/6oz/1½ cups all-purpose flour
A pinch of salt
75g/3oz/⅓ cup butter, softened, or shredded suet
50g/2oz/¼ cup superfine sugar
1 egg
About 6 tbsp milk

To serve
Extra corn syrup
Custard

You can make this as one pudding or individual puddings, if you prefer, in which case reduce the cooking time to about 1–1¼ hours. In the microwave, a large pudding will take about 7 minutes.

1. Grease a 1.2 litre/2pt pudding basin and spoon the syrup into it.
2. Put the flour and salt in a bowl and mix in the softened butter or suet and the sugar. Make a well in the center.
3. Add the egg and start to mix it into the dry ingredients, adding the milk as you do so in order to give a soft consistency that drops off the spoon easily. You may need a little more or less milk.
4. Spoon the mixture into the basin. Cover with pleated waxed paper and secure with string. Place in a large pan and pour boiling water around the basin to come halfway up the sides of the basin. Cover and steam for 1½ hours, topping up with boiling water as necessary. The pudding should be risen and a knife inserted in the center should come out clean.
5. Serve hot with some extra warmed syrup to pour over, if liked, and hot custard.

Serves 4

175g/6oz/1½ cups all-purpose flour
150g/5oz/⅔ cup sweet butter, diced
100g/4oz/½ cup superfine sugar
1 egg yolk
About 3 tbsp water
900g/2lb pears, peeled, cored,
and halved

To serve
A little light cream, if liked

Pear tarte tatin

A classic French dessert, this is usually made with dessert apples but using pears instead makes a lovely alternative version. It is cooked upside down, so you turn it out to reveal the caramelized fruit which becomes the top of the tart.

1. Put the flour in a bowl and add half the butter. Rub in until the mixture resembles breadcrumbs.
2. Stir in 1 tbsp of sugar. Mix in the egg yolk and enough cold water to make a firm dough.
3. Wrap the dough in plastic wrap and chill while you prepare the pears.
4. Heat the oven to 190°C/375°F/Gas 5 and grease a deep 20cm/8in pie dish.
5. Melt the remaining butter and sugar

together and drizzle over the base of the dish. Arrange the pear halves attractively on top.
6. Roll out the pastry to just slightly larger than the pan and place it over the pears, tucking in the edges.
7. Bake in the oven for about 30 minutes until the pastry is cooked through
8. Invert carefully on to a serving plate and serve hot or cold, with a little pouring cream, if liked.

Baked rice pudding

Cinnamon has been chosen to complement the creamy flavor of this rice pudding, with a decorative cinnamon stick to serve. Your guests will either love or hate the crisp skin that forms on the top, so reserve that for those who will enjoy it.

Serves 4

50g/2oz/¼ cup pudding rice
2 tbsp superfine sugar
600ml/1pt/2½ cups milk
15g/½oz/1 tbsp butter
1 cinnamon stick, broken in half
1 tsp vanilla extract
A pinch of ground cinnamon

1. Heat the oven to 160°C/325°F/Gas 3 and butter an ovenproof dish.
2. Sprinkle the rice and sugar into the dish, then pour in the milk and add the butter, half the cinnamon stick, and the vanilla extract.
3. Bake in the oven for about 2 hours until cooked through and creamy with a crisp skin on the top.
4. Reserve the skin for those who like it, and serve the pudding sprinkled with a little ground cinnamon and decorated with the remaining piece of cinnamon.

Rhubarb crumble

This is a traditional crumble mix, but you can add or substitute ingredients to give you more variety. Try it with some crushed ginger biscuits, rolled oats, oatmeal, brown sugar or crushed macaroons. Vary the fruit, too, or use a mixture.

Serves 4

900g/2lb rhubarb, cut into
1cm/½in chunks
2 tbsp water
150g/5oz/⅔ cup superfine sugar
175g/6oz/1½ cups all-purpose flour
½ tsp ground ginger
75g/3oz/⅓ cup butter
2 tbsp demerara sugar

To serve
Whipped cream or ice-cream

1. Heat the oven to 190°C/375°F/Gas 5 and grease a deep baking dish.
2. Spoon the rhubarb into the dish and sprinkle with the water and half the superfine sugar.
3. Mix the flour and ginger in a bowl and stir in the remaining sugar. Rub in the butter until the mixture resembles coarse breadcrumbs.
4. Sprinkle the crumble mix over the rhubarb, then sprinkle with the demerara sugar.
5. Bake in the oven for about 30 minutes until crisp and golden.
6. Serve warm or cold with cream or ice-cream.